INTERNATIONAL McCORMICK TRACTORS

Reliable Red: Farmall, Deering and Case-International

Henry Rasmussen

Motorbooks International
Publishers & Wholesalers
®

First published in 1989 by Motorbooks International Publishers & Wholesalers, Inc, P O Box 2, 729 Prospect Avenue, Osceola, WI 54020 USA

© Henry Rasmussen, 1989
Reprinted fall 1992

Printed and bound in Hong Kong

The information in this book is true and complete to the best of our knowledge. All recommendations are made without any guarantee on the part of the author or publisher, who also disclaim any liability incurred in connection with the use of this data or specific details

We recognize that some words, model names and designations, for example, mentioned herein are the property of the trademark holder. We use them for identification purposes only. This is not an official publication

Library of Congress Cataloging-in-Publication Data
ISBN 0-87938-372-0

Motorbooks International books are also available at discounts in bulk quantity for industrial or sales-promotional use. For details write to Special Sales Manager at the Publisher's address

On the front cover: Richard Harmon of Vista, California, puts his freshly restored 1945 Farmall A to the test. **On the back cover:** *A rare 1937 McCormick-Deering W-12.* **On the frontispiece:** *The McCormick-Deering logo, here decorating the radiator of a W-30.* **On the title page:** *The day's work is over—a mid-fifties Farmall 300 has come to rest in the field.* **On this page:** *An elaborate maze of plumbing faced the operator of a 1910 International.* **On the following spread:** *A row of 1929 International TracTracTor T-20s.* **On the last page:** *A common sight on the twenties farm—the red wheels and gray hood of McCormick-Deering's popular 15-30, this one of an early, 1922 vintage.*

Contents

Introduction

From revolutionary reaper to International Harvester

The Nineteenth Century saw not only the germination of the agricultural implement industry as such, but also the explosive growth that followed. Ultimately, during the latter part of the period, the field sprouted such a rich flora of enterprises—and such fierce competition—that the soil could barely nourish them all.

The most vigorous plant to emerge from this plethora was the International Harvester Company, whose two major roots, the McCormick Harvesting Machine Company and the Deering Harvester Company, were joined in 1902. The former was founded by Cyrus Hall McCormick, an inventor credited with the perfection of the reaper, and the latter by William Deering, whose organization pioneered the development of the binder.

With the amalgamation of these two corporate giants, both Chicago based, the stage was set for further expansion, in terms of products as well as markets. Europe and the rest of the world would now benefit from the inventions that had revolutionized life on the North American farm.

In the early twenties, International further advanced its position of leadership with the development of the all-purpose tractor, the Farmall. This machine spawned generation upon generation of new tractors—an offspring destined to populate the earth.

Today, after eight decades of activity in the field, hardly an acre has escaped cultivation by the machines from International. It is a tribute to the loyalty of the farmer, and the longevity of the product, that the aging machines still serve ably alongside the new.

An era when giants roamed the earth

In the late 1800s, development of farm machinery reached a point where no improvements seemed possible—progress was hampered by the horse, with its restrictions on power and speed.

Enter the steam traction engine. Yet unfortunately the bulk of this machine, coupled with the cost of manufacture, resulted in limited usefulness.

The advent of the internal combustion engine finally broke the deadlock. The Deering people built their first stationary gasoline unit in 1891. In the McCormick shops, similar experiments led to the Auto-Mover, introduced in 1898.

It was not until 1906 that International became seriously involved with tractor manufacture. Just fourteen units were built that year. The next year, production rose to around 150 units and in 1908 more than 600 were completed. The tractor had arrived.

The earliest Internationals used the company's own Famous engine, while the rest of the machinery came from an outside source in the form of the Morton traction truck.

In 1907, International introduced a tractor of its own construction. With further refinement came fancy names: one, the Mogul, was sold through McCormick dealers; another, the Titan, was marketed by the Deering network.

Progress now grew rapidly. Yet since the basic construction followed that of the huge steam traction engines, the early tractors were still giants—some weighing as much as 20,000 pounds.

With production soon in the thousands, International swiftly established itself as a leader in the field, capturing no less than a third of the market share.

An unrestored survivor from the heavy metal era, the 1910 International shown on the previous page exemplifies the company's earliest efforts. While the first model featured forward and reverse friction drive, the Type A, introduced in 1907, was equipped with a single-speed, gear-forward and friction-reverse system. Later, improved versions— Types A, B and C—used gear drive both forward and reverse, in addition to two-speed transmissions. The maximum speed was a rip-roaring 2 mph! Shown here is a 20 hp, early Type A. The model was produced until 1911; 607 units were built. Of these, 248 came from the Upper Sandusky plant, while the remainder originated in the Akron Works. Power came from the 250 rpm, horizontal, single-cylinder Famous engine, boasting a 9 inch bore and a 15 inch stroke. The Internationals of this era used an evaporative cooling system— a bird's-eye view is seen to the left. Pictured above, a close-up of the steering pivot. On the following spread, the machine shows off its majestic proportions. The twin flywheels measure 50 inches. Notice the belt pulley, with its hand-operated clutch. The rear wheels stand six feet tall. Weight? In excess of 13,500 pounds!

Mass production spells cheaper and smaller

The huge Moguls and Titans were really only sensible for use on the open prairie. Even here the awkwardness of sheer size and weight soon relegated these giants—like the steam traction engines before them—to stationary work.

While the limited usefulness of the early tractors was brought home by the pioneer farmers, other factors further accentuated the need for reducing the size of the machine: the effects of World War I were felt on the farm in lack of manpower and increased demand for grain to feed the hungry. Smaller and cheaper was the answer.

International's foray into this market, the 8-16 Mogul, limited to a run of fourteen units, arrived in 1914. In the next three years the total jumped to 14,000 units! By the end of production, in 1919, the similar 10-20 Mogul had added another 9,000 units. The Mogul was replaced by the 8-16 International, of which 33,000 units were built between 1917 and 1922.

The winner in terms of numbers was the 10-20 Titan. From a humble beginning in 1915, when just seven units were built, production swelled dramatically in the next few years. A total of 78,000 units had been manufactured by the end of production in 1922.

The secret behind these numbers was not just more versatile tractors, but also lower prices. In 1910, a Type B Mogul carried a tag of $2,200, while in 1922, an 8-16 International could be had for $670— with a two-bottom plow thrown in for good measure.

By the late teens, the tractor—with International among the front runners—was on its way to conquering the American farm.

An exquisitely restored 1915 Mogul 8-16 shows off its attractive green and red color scheme in the photograph on the previous spread. At this point, power came from a horizontal, single-cylinder engine, equipped with low tension magneto ignition. Pictured above, the workplace of the Mogul 8-16. The two levers activate reverse and forward gears—only one forward speed was provided. Braking is accomplished by rotating the small wheel seen immediately to the left of the driver's seat. Throttle? There is none! Since it was governor controlled, the Mogul operated at just one engine speed. To the left, an overhead view, effectively illustrating the narrow tread of the tractor. The close-set front wheels allowed unimpeded belt operation, as well as an outstanding turning radius—a feature appreciated by the buyers of the new Mogul, who were often owners of smaller farms. The photograph also invites a closer examination of the simple worm-and-sector steering mechanism.

This 8-16 Mogul, an older restoration, spends its retirement years in the care of Nevada's Ponderosa Ranch. Here, the old-timer is surrounded by a collection of antique stoves. The year of production is unclear, but is believed to be 1916; this conclusion is reached by judging the difference in design between the clutch wheel of the machine featured here and the 1915 Mogul 8-16 pictured previously. Earlier Moguls were equipped with a solid wheel, while later versions sported a spoked type. Only twenty units were built in 1914. Full production commenced in 1915, with 5,111 units emerging from the Chicago Tractor Works. The 8-16 used a hopper-type cooling system. The stack on top of the hopper is a vent and expansion outlet for the evaporating cooling water. Only a faint mist could be seen escaping during operation, and not, as in the case of the steam engines, a massive cloud of smoke and steam. On the 8-16, the fuel tank was located near the rear axle. On the improved 10-20, the tank was moved to the top of the transmission case. Among the mechanical improvements on this model, available as late as 1919, was the two-speed transmission, with the gears running in a constant bath of oil.

Two of the mechanical wonders dramatically improving life on the farm during the early part of our century, the truck and the tractor, are captured in this view from California's Sacramento Valley. Ford's Model T is of a 1925 vintage, while International's Titan is from 1919. The Titan represented another step on the road to creating a smaller tractor. This machine, built at the Milwaukee Works—in larger numbers than any other tractor to date—weighed only one fourth of the largest early Internationals, or 5,700 pounds. Power came from a horizontal, twin-cylinder, kerosene-burning unit, reaching its peak at 500 rpm. Two forward gears were provided. Top speed was still not much to brag about—just under 3 mph. The beautifully restored example shown here does not feature fenders, probably an optional item, which were found on most Titans. On the early model, the fenders were short, while a full-length type became available on the second version, introduced in 1919. The following page offers another view of the machine. The prominent tank mounted above the front wheels does not contain fuel, but cooling water. Consequently, due to the use of the thermosyphon system, there was no need for a fan or pump.

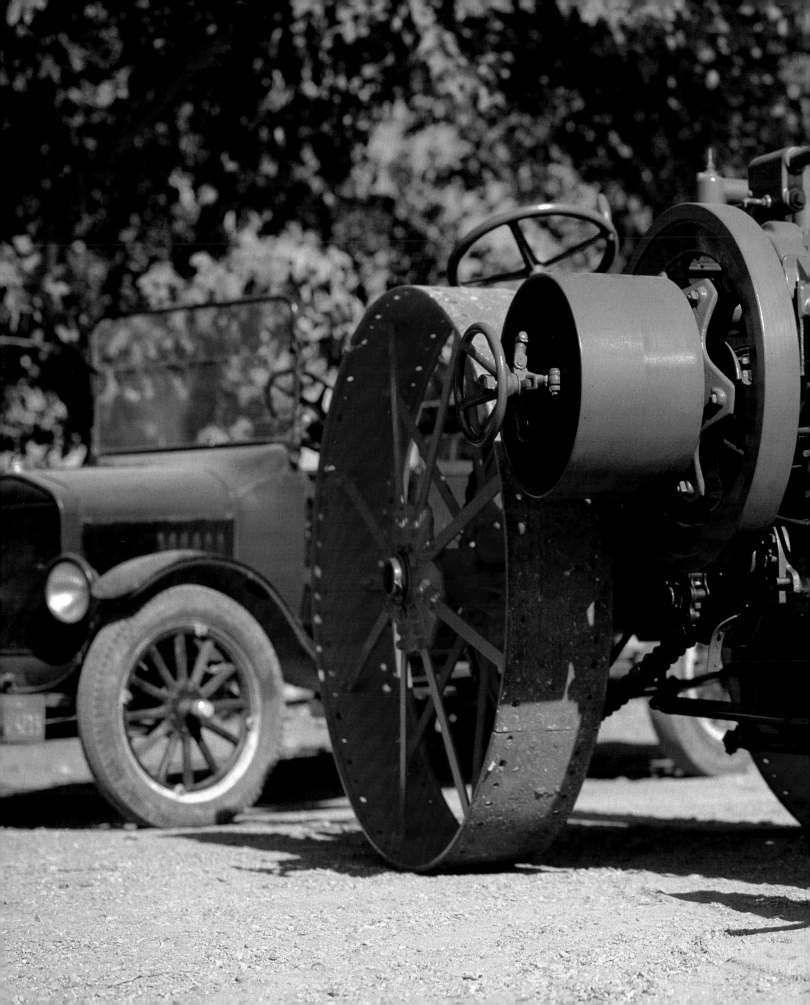

With the use of gray for the main body and red for the wheels, the Titan pioneered a color scheme that would characterize International's products throughout the twenties and much of the thirties. In the photograph above, the camera focuses attention on the Titan's governor, with the clutch to the left of it, and the magneto to the right, covered by a leather pouch. Pictured to the right, the Titan's rear wheel. Early Moguls used round spokes, while early Titans used flat ones. The latter soon became the standard and remained in style until the arrival of rubber tires in the early thirties.

Notice the roller chain—this method for transmission of power was used on many of the early Internationals. With the arrival of the all-new 15-30 McCormick-Deering came the final drive system of the modern tractor. Production of the Titan reached 2,246 units in 1916, the first year. A peak was attained in 1918, with 17,675 units emerging—at this rate, a new Titan was started every 4 1/2 minutes. In the course of the sales war with Ford, during which the Fordson was for a time marketed at a price below production cost, the Titan sold for $700. In 1921, the price had risen to $1,200.

Contrasted with a backdrop of
rusting workhorses, this restored
late-model International 8-16 looks
as good as new. The 8-16 was first
seen in 1917, when just 38 units
emerged from the Chicago Tractor
Works, where production remained
during the entire run. The 8-16
represents yet another effort by
International's engineers to down-
size the tractor and evolve its design.
Of special interest is the heavy
influence of truck and automotive
design, as was the fashion for a time.
Like International's trucks, this
tractor had its radiator mounted
behind the engine, and also featured
a sloping hood, much like its road-
going counterpart. This feature must
have been viewed by the farmer as an
important advancement as it
certainly improved vision. The power
source of the 8-16 was a four-cylinder
unit, similar in design to the engine
mounted in the firm's Model G
trucks. Unlike the trucks, the final
drive of the tractor was by dual roller
chains. The transmission featured
three forward gears. At 4 mph, top
speed was increased over earlier and
contemporary models. Pictured on
the previous spread is a 1918
vintage, a year when 3,162 units
were manufactured.

During the five-year production run of the 8-16 International, a number of design changes were implemented. The first series, running from 1917 to 1919, carries a VB prefix. The second generation, built from 1919 to 1921, features an identification plaque stamped with an HC prefix. From the exterior, this model can be recognized by a water-type air cleaner. The IC series came in 1922, the last year of production, when 7,506 units were manufactured. With this model came a final relocation of both the air cleaner and the exhaust pipe. The photographs on this spread illustrate the evolution as it effected the left side of the engine, with its manifold and carburetor. To the right, a restored HC, strikingly decorative in its straightforward simplicity. Above, an unrestored VB, decidedly more primal and cluttered. The small, notched device seen on the rectangular manifold of the VB is the heat indicator control. A similar-looking device, found on the pipe attached to the carburetor of the HC, does not have the same function—in this case it is the choke lever. The 8-16 constitutes an important link in the chain that brought the tractor from a basic, steam traction contraption to a modern machine.

The coming of age

Bitter competition gives birth to the modern tractor

The next milestone in tractor development was not erected by International, but by Ford. On the heels of the Model T, which had placed the automobile within reach of the average family, came the Fordson tractor, introduced in 1917. This machine, with its manageable size and advanced construction (the frame consisted of a two-piece casting, bolted together in the middle) revolutionized tractor design.

At International, the engineers were immediately sent back to the drawing board, charged with the assignment of creating a new line of tractors that would recapture the number one spot on the sales charts. The position had been relinquished to the Fordson, which, with the advantage of a nationwide automotive dealer network, had by 1920 sold as many as 100,000 units.

It was not until 1921 that International could introduce the result of its effort: the McCormick-Deering 15-30. Ending the era of heavyweight International tractors, this machine—completely new, from radiator to rear wheels—went one up on the Fordson, featuring a one-piece cast-iron frame.

Next in line came a smaller brother of the 15-30, the 10-20, introduced in 1923. The 10-20 was to become one of the most popular tractors of the twenties and thirties. In production until 1934, the 15-30 was reproduced 160,000 times, while the 10-20—remaining in the catalog until 1939—reached a total of 215,000.

The soundness of competition and a free marketplace had been proven once again, as had the mettle of the International Harvester engineers and salesforce. The number one spot had been recaptured.

With the McCormick-Deering 15-30, the modern tractor took its place in the International product line. The photograph on the previous page illustrates the new look, featuring a perfectly restored example from 1922. This marked the second year of production, when the Milwaukee Works completed 1,350 units, compared to 199 in 1921. In 1923, the figure was 4,886. From the front-mounted radiator to the squared-off hood and the one-piece frame, the 15-30 was all new. The idea was to enclose all parts, protecting them from dirt and wear. In this photograph, featuring the right-hand facade of the 15-30 engine—a vertical, four-cylinder, 1000 rpm unit—the uncluttered design is evident. Inside, the crankshaft featured ball bearing mains for the first time. Removable sleeves were another advance, making overhaul an easier and less costly undertaking. Yet another feature was the addition of a power takeoff—an $8.50 option—which allowed implements to be driven through the shaft and no longer depend on their own engines, drive wheels and belts. In 1927, a 15-30 cost $1,250. In 1928, at the peak of its popularity, production of the 15-30 soared to 35,525 units.

With the 10-20 McCormick-Deering (captured in the scene on the previous page) International's engineers and marketing men hit the nail right on the head. The little machine was just the ticket for the small farm, and the model remained in the International catalog throughout most of the twenties and thirties. Production reached a peak in 1929, the vintage of our featured example. The output that year marked a new production high for International, with close to 40,000 units coming off the line. The 10-20 was simply a down-sized 15-30, with an overall length of 123 inches—14 inches less than its big brother— which greatly improved maneuverability. All the important features of the 15-30, such as the four-cylinder engine with a 4 1/2 inch bore and a 5 inch stroke, a one-piece frame, a belt pulley and full-length fenders, were also found on the 10-20. As with the early examples of the 15-30, the 10-20 at first used a water-type air cleaner, while later examples of both tractors featured a Pomona oil-type unit. Seen here are details of the 10-20. To the right, the throttle and spark retardation levers. Above, the sediment bowl, mounted immediately underneath the fuel tank.

The picture on this page was photographed on the premises of the Ponderosa Ranch, located in Incline Village, Nevada. Established in 1967, the site was used for the filming of many an episode in television's popular Bonanza series. Thanks to the efforts of founder William Anderson, the ranch features vast collections of memorabilia from the old days of the West, including numerous tractors and other farm equipment. Although many of these machines sit unprotected from the elements (a fact causing the serious collector some discomfort) the museum is well worth a visit. The Ponderosa display includes an example of McCormick-Deering's W-30. Introduced in 1932, this model was positioned between the 10-20 and the 15-30, a fact reflected in the price list: $875 for the 10-20, $975 for the W-30 and $1,100 for the 15-30—or 22-36, as this tractor was often referred to toward the end of its long life.

Sharing space with its Fordson stable mate on a farm in Sweden, the W-30 captured in this photograph has its radiator covered with a row of vertical louvers, a feature designed to keep those icy winds (so prevalent in these latitudes) from lowering engine temperature during winter operation. Notice that the angle of the louvers could be adjusted from the driver's seat. This tractor, of a 1938 vintage, was purchased new by the grandparents of Bjorn Waldegard, who would subsequently attain world renown for his successes on the international rally circuit. Having served on the family farm for many years, and having passed from hand to hand in the local farm community, the surviving W-30 finally ended up in the care of the Sandquist brothers—Kjell and Lars-Eric—who administered the restoration. The brothers are founders of a rapidly growing Swedish tractor club. The blue Volvo PV 444, sticking its familiar nose into the picture, adds authenticity to the atmosphere. The brothers' use of red for the repainting of the tractor is correct, since at this point International had changed over from the gray that had characterized its products for so long.

Boasting one of the lowest production runs of the thirties International tractors, the small W-12 has become a most attractive commodity to collectors. The example in the photographs on this spread, originates from 1934, the first year of manufacture. Peak production was reached in 1937, with 1,032 units being built that year. The model was replaced in 1938, after 3,617 had been completed, by the W-14. This model was essentially the same as the W-12, except that engine speed had been raised from 1400 rpm to 1650 rpm. The engine was the identical four-cylinder unit used in the regular F-12 Farmall line. The W-14 lasted until 1940, adding another 2,162 units to the grand total. Rolling on steel wheels, the W-12 carried a price tag of $725. Rubber was available, but at extra cost. Some farmers simply cut the treads of truck tires to fit over the steel wheels, as shown in the picture to the left. The W-12 was an extremely attractive little tractor, equipped with a versatile drawbar as well as a most useful power takeoff—shown in the picture above. The PTO was included, but if the buyer wanted a belt pulley, another $35 was added to the bill.

The W-12 was available in an orchard version, designated O-12. The narrow tread made it suited for this type of work. Three forward gears provided a selection of speeds: 2 1/2, 3 1/4 and 7 1/2 mph. Between 1935 and 1938, 2,386 units were manufactured. The similar O-14, available in 1938 and 1939, added 639 copies. To make matters more complicated—and intriguing—for the collector, the same tractors came equipped for industrial use, then labeled I-12 and I-14. But that is not the end of the story. The O-12 and O-14 were also available for use on golf courses, when a Fairway designation was used. Pictured here is an O-12 of unknown vintage; accurate identification was not possible. The unique survivor unfortunately sports an alien color scheme.

The biggest International during the latter half of the thirties was McCormick-Deering's W-40. The unrestored survivor pictured here is of 1934 vintage, the first year of production. Manufacture ended in 1940, after 6,454 units had been built. The W-40 featured a six-cylinder engine, the same unit also powering International trucks of the period. A close examination of the engine reveals the diamond logo cast into the block. This tractor sports factory-original rubber wheels. Equipped this way, the price tag was $1,611 in 1940, $306 higher than when steel wheels were employed. The tractor was also available in a diesel version. When introduced in 1934, the WD-40 was the first American wheel-type tractor to feature this type of power. The gasoline version produced 32 hp at the drawbar, while the diesel version boosted output an additional 5 hp. When production ended in 1940, 3,370 units had been built. Considering the significance of this machine, coupled with its scarcity, the WD-40 is one of the most collectible of the period. The enthusiast with a taste for the ultimate would probably crave an ID-40—the industrial version—of which just 238 units were made!

48

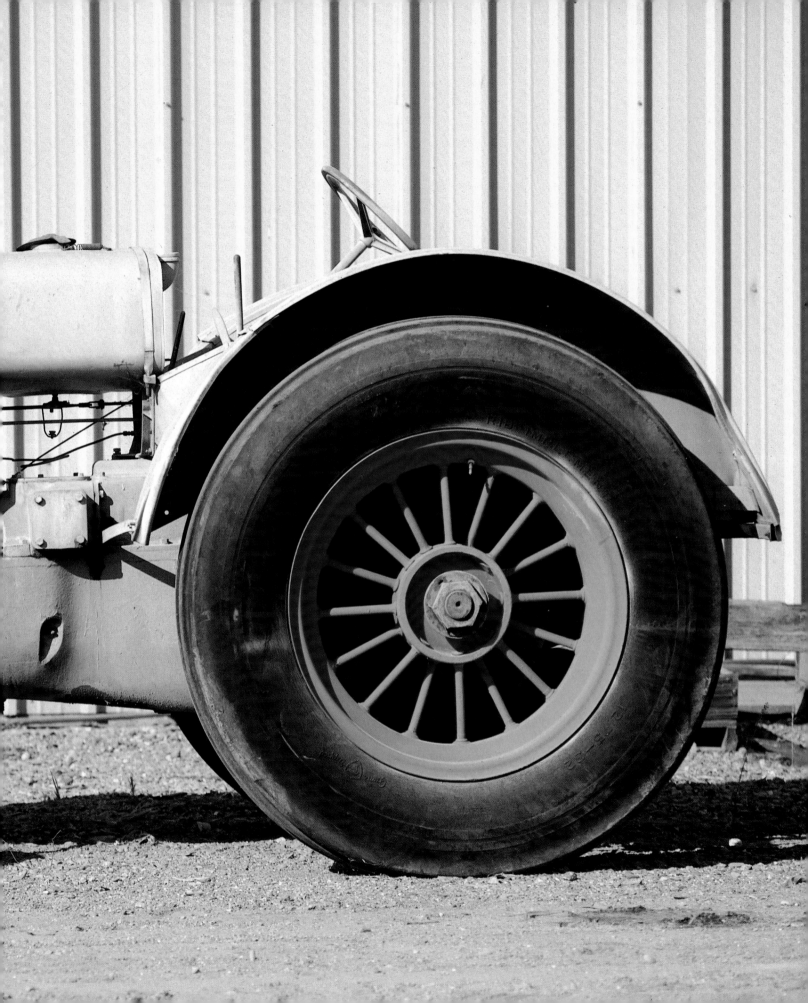

For 1940, International's McCormick-Deering line received the same streamlined styling as had already been bestowed on the Farmall line in 1939. A number of models were available, ranging in size from the standard-tread W-4, to the three-bottom plow W-6, to the 52 hp W-9. In 1945 (the Deering name had by then been dropped from the name plaque) the company offered special versions of the W-9 and the WD-9 for use by rice growers. These versions were designated WR-9 and WDR-9, respectively. An example of the diesel version is shown here. The rare machine was found high in the Sierra Nevada mountains. It was certainly a long way from the rice fields of California's Sacramento Valley, where it most likely served during the early part of its life. For heavy-duty applications, the model featured extra-wide tires. In addition, the rears could be doubled-up. Wider fenders was another option. In order to extend the hours of operation into the night, a pair of headlights was included as part of the package. The long hours also required that the comfort of the driver be improved—a padded deluxe seat was furnished. Production of the special rice model ended in 1953.

A tractor for every farm and all purposes

Already in the early teens, manufacturers began wrestling with the problem of creating a tractor able to handle all the chores on the farm. In 1915, International introduced a motor cultivator, but the contraption was not well received, and production ended in 1919.

For a long time it was gospel that two types of machines were needed. First, a larger tractor to be used for heavier duties such as plowing. Second, a smaller type to be used for lighter chores such as row crop cultivation. Unfortunately, there was a catch. The average farmer could simply not afford two tractors.

The search for an all-purpose design became a priority, particularly as the notion of the horseless farm became increasingly popular. The horse, after all, was an expensive proposition, consuming food whether in use or not, and occupying valuable grazing land.

International finally scored with its Farmall, introduced in 1922. Its release was limited in the first years, as the new design underwent thorough testing. Full production commenced in 1926, when the Farmall Works in Rock Island, Illinois, opened its doors. The success of the Farmall was immediate—in 1930, International celebrated the completion of its 100,000th unit.

Another figure illustrating the impact of the Farmall—and the imitators that inevitably followed—is found in the relationship between the number of tractors and horses on the farm. In 1920, tractors totaled 200,000, horses 25 million. In 1940, the figure for tractors had increased nearly tenfold, while the number of horses had been cut in half.

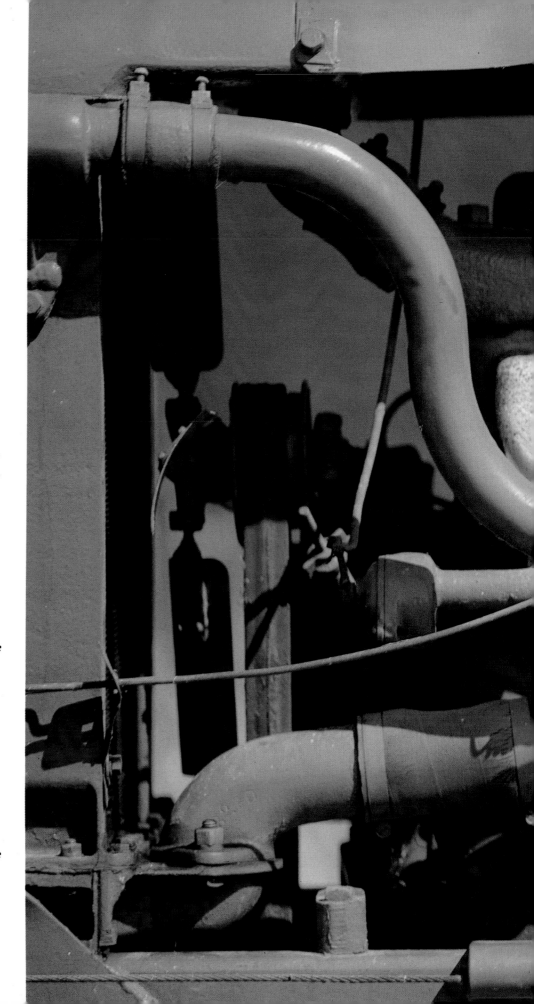

The Farmall (the previous spread shows a 1927 vintage) was the brainchild of International engineer Bert Benjamin, whose patient efforts paid off in a big way. After a slow start, during which the company had trouble meeting demand, the line finally began to move with the opening of the new Rock Island facility. Still, only 4,430 units were built in 1926. In 1927, the figure swelled to 9,502. And by 1930, 200 units came off the line every day! In Benjamin's first experimental units, the engine was mounted crosswise. In the final Farmall shape, the engine was placed parallel with the frame, which was not cast, but of a ladder type manufactured from tubular steel. Power came from a four-cylinder, 1200 rpm unit, featuring a 3 3/4 inch bore and a 5 inch stroke. The left side of the engine is shown here. Note the minimal exhaust pipe. The Farmall's tricycle design was a crucial element of its appeal, with the small, close-set front wheels able to run between the crops. Three forward speeds and one reverse were provided. As in the following photograph, the rear axle had also been designed with the row-crop farmer in mind, providing ample clearance.

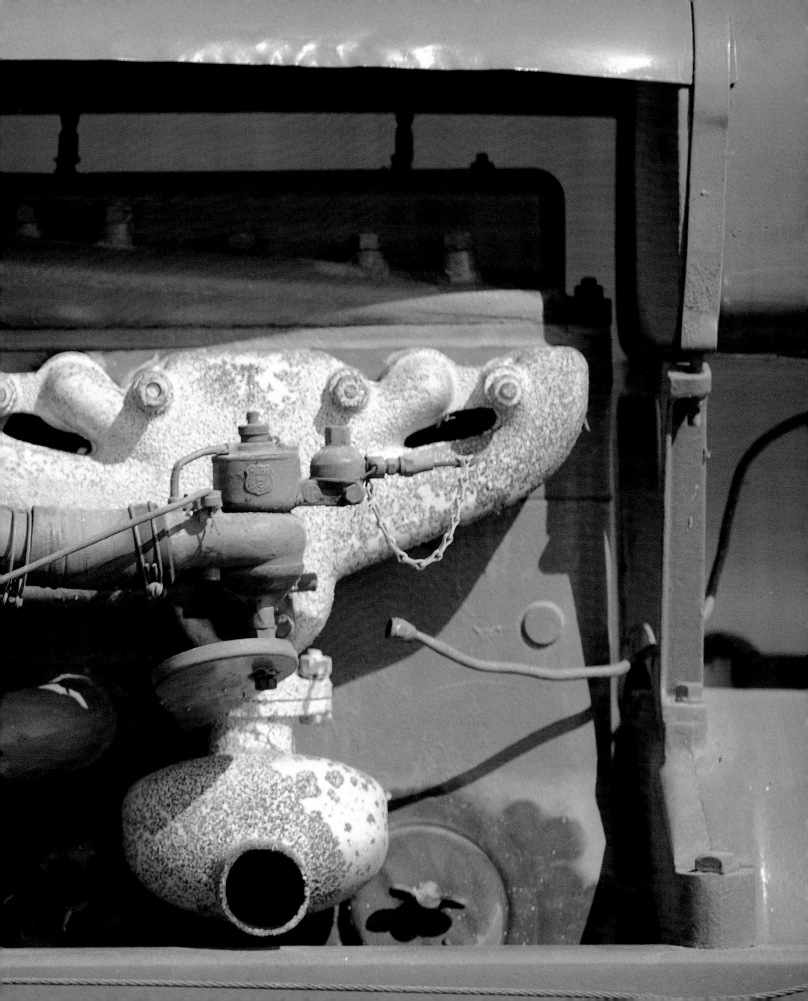

The Farmall featured a vertical steering wheel, with the axle running horizontally across the hood to a worm-and-sector arrangement, looking much like the system used on the earlier 8-16 Mogul. For versatility, implement attachment points were provided up front, in the middle and in the back. Another feature was a system whereby, when the steering wheel was turned all the way, the rear brake on that side became automatically activated. This was accomplished through wires running the length of each side of the frame. One of the pulleys for this system can be seen immediately ahead of the brace connecting the radiator frame with the steering column. This brace, by the way, is not stock, but was the work of a previous owner, who must have found it necessary to stabilize the column. Otherwise, the machine is completely stock—although the restorer never got around to attaching the decals, one on each side of the tank. Shown here is an example of nature's artwork—half a decade of exposure to the elements has had an intriguing effect. Today, it is difficult to imagine that the lettering was once white on a black background.

The F-20, introduced in 1932, was a further refinement of the original Farmall. The old model subsequently became known as the Regular, and was phased out as the F-20 took its place on the assembly line. The new model, which would soon shatter the production record set by the old, had become slightly larger than the one it replaced. While the engine and its dimensions remained unchanged, the F-20 offered approximately ten percent more power. The additional horses were transmitted via a fourth forward gear, with a top speed of 3 3/4 mph. Tested in Nebraska, the F-20 produced 16 hp at the drawbar and 24 hp at the belt. The 1933 model featured here is—after more than half a century of uninterrupted service—still going strong. With its cotton planter attachment, its massive propane tank and its heavy-duty wheel weights, the machine looks every bit the part. Notice that the steering mechanism has become fully enclosed. In 1935, the F-20 carried a price tag of $895. That year, 26,295 units were built, which was nearly one-fifth of the total number of wheel-type tractors produced in the nation.

The F-30, introduced one year before the F-20, was the largest of the second-generation Farmalls. It sported a 94 inch wheelbase and weighed 5,300 pounds. Only 623 units were built the initial year; in 1932, the first full year of manufacture, production rose to 3,122 units. The example featured in the photograph to the left—spotted in a barn in California's Salinas Valley—is of unspecified vintage and features a single front wheel. The rubber rears appear to be factory originals, an option adding up to a tag of $1,225. In the photograph above is another unusual F-30. The machine features a high-clearance front axle attachment, developed for sugar cane cultivation. As part of the original design, the rear wheels could be moved as far apart as 96 inches. The closest setting was 68 inches. The survivor was photographed in the backyard of the Mickey Grove Museum in Lodi, California, where it awaits restoration. The serial number, FB 21812, reveals it to be a 1937 model. This was the year after the Farmall tractors donned a new suit: in 1936 the gray was replaced by red, a color that has since become the shade universally synonymous with International tractors and its implements.

The photographs on this and the following pages feature a Farmall F-14. The F-14 was a short-lived model—coming on the heels of the F-12—produced only in 1938 and 1939. As with all collector markets, the trading in tractors is ruled by supply and demand, and the F-14 has become much sought after. In the first year, 15,609 units were produced. The figure for 1939 was 11,787. The F-14 was similar to the F-12 in virtually all aspects, except for the engine, which peaked at 1650 rpm instead of 1200 rpm. At $720, the wide-front version seen in these pictures cost $65 more than its narrow-front counterpart. This tractor was photographed in Sweden, where it has lived all its life. The machine is in a highly preferred state; since it has always been stored indoors, the original paint is still intact. The first-ever overseas factory was established in Sweden, where the small city of Norrkoping was chosen as a plant site in 1904. On the following page is a close-up of the F-14 engine. Famous Swedish ingenuity has been applied to the problem of keeping the brittle old hoses from bursting.

An unstoppable spread of Farmall red

In the late thirties, industrial design became an important tool in capturing larger market shares. And with industrial design came streamlining. The square, cluttered radiator area of the tractor now became smooth and round. Flowing lines were also bestowed on a number of other parts, such as the hood and fenders.

A new color scheme had already in the mid-thirties become yet another means for the stylists to achieve a new look. The combination of gray and red, as established on the classic Internationals, had been replaced by a bright red. This became the look of the quintessential Farmall—a look that still decorates the fields and barnyards of the agricultural landscape all over the world.

But the attention to the exterior did not mean that the interior was neglected. Even the smallest tractor came with power takeoff and belt pulley. And new features got fancy names, such as Culti-Vision, which stood for an offset hood that gave the farmer vastly improved vision while cultivating the crop.

The line was so versatile that every size and need was catered to—from the vegetable grower and the small Cub to the midwestern grain farmer and the massive M.

Production numbers reflected this variety. The A and Super A, built from 1939 to 1954, totaled 220,000 units. The tally for the H, produced between 1939 and 1953, was 390,000. The C and the Super C, manufactured from 1948 to 1954, added another 170,000. The M, built between 1939 and 1952, totaled 300,000. Counting the Cub and a number of McCormick models, International tractor production soared into the millions.

The beautiful tractor showing off its streamlined body in the pictures on the previous pages—photographed on the premises of the Antique Gas & Steam Engine Museum in Vista, California—is the beloved and versatile little A, which was the smallest unit in the new Farmall class, introduced in 1939. The A was designed for one-row work. Its four-cylinder engine, featuring a 3 inch bore and a 4 inch stroke, and reaching its power peak at 1400 rpm, produced 16 hp at the drawbar and 18 hp at the belt. Also found in the Farmall line were the B and C models, a C pictured here. The B, built between 1939 and 1947, was powered by the same engine used in the A, but was capable of straddling a wider range of rows. The A featured distances from 40 to 68 inches, while the B could handle 64 to 92 inches. The C, shown here, featured the same engine as the A and the B, but was built on the same frame as the H and M. The Culti-Vision feature was maintained, but the steering column was mounted at a sharper angle, resulting in a more horizontal steering wheel position.

Designed to pull a three-bottom plow, the M was the biggest and most powerful member of the Farmall family. It can be said that the M meant to International in the post–World War II era what the original Farmall meant in the twenties—both were immensely popular and reached higher production figures than any International tractor before them. The base price in 1940 was $1,112. Power output was 34 hp measured at the drawbar, and 39 hp measured at the belt. Weight was just over 5,000 pounds. When production ended in 1952, the Super M prolonged the lifespan of the beloved machine by two years. The Super M could be equipped with a Torque Amplifier, a unit that changed the speed range at the pull of a lever. The standard range was otherwise broad, with the five-speed transmission providing speeds between 3 and 17 mph. Diesel power was also available in the form of the MD. The M featured here is a 1946 model. On the day it had its picture taken, the old workhorse used its PTO to power a hay chopper. On the following page, a 1950 BM, built in Great Britain, has found its way to faraway Sweden, where a future farmer seems thrilled with the prospect of soon being able to run it for real.

With the end of the letter series in 1954, International introduced the number series which meant, due to the frequency of the development cycle, a certain amount of confusion for today's collector. The 100, a replacement for the B, was designed to pull one 16 inch plow or two 12 inch plows. The 200, with its 21 hp at the drawbar and 24 hp at the belt, was the next step up. The 300, the three-plow machine, was the replacement for the M. But there was also a utility 300. Then there was the 400, capable of 45 hp at the drawbar and 51 hp at the belt. And there was the standard tread W-400, and the diesel-powered W-400D. At the top of the line was the 600, built only in 1956. After that year, International changed numbers again. The 100 was replaced by the 130. The 200 became the 230, as shown on the previous pages with Norman Martin at the wheel. The 300 became the 330—but no, it became the 350! Then there was the 450, and the biggest, the 650. In 1958 came new styling and new numbers. This machine is a 200 from 1956. After more than three decades of service, the old faithful is still going strong, but performing only light chores now, such as carrying a load of milk to the pampered calves on a dairy farm.

The owner of a new Farmall 300 could pride himself on having purchased one of the most advanced tractors of the day. The Farmall Fast-Hitch, for example, was a fully hydraulic system that allowed easy implement attachment. The Farmall Torque Amplifier was another innovation, providing a shift-free choice of two speeds in each gear for a total of ten speeds. The pristine 300 splashing the viewer with a handsome broadside of red on the previous page dates from 1956. It stands as a perfect example of the economy of older Farmalls. The present owner bought it a few years ago for $800.

After putting $1,500 into a restoration, the machine is as good as new, ready to perform ably for another couple of decades. On this spread, left, the workplace of the 300. The frenzy of the fifties automotive styling war had spilled over to the tractor market, with the Farmall receiving its own little dashboard, as well as an elaborate horn button. Above, with the introduction of the number series came a new symbol. The old International logo had served since the formation of the company in 1902. The new one was unveiled in 1945, but did not take its place of pride on the crest of the hood until 1954.

Fall is in the air—and in the soil. The scene reproduced here, photographed in Wisconsin, depicts a 1955 Farmall 400 coupled to a harrow. A break in the proceedings gave the photographer a chance to capture the old workhorse in the process of helping the farmer prepare the soil for the winter. The gasoline version of the 400 produced 45 hp at the drawbar and 51 hp at the belt. This generous amount of power came from a 2000 rpm, four-cylinder unit featuring a 4 inch bore and a 5 1/4 inch stroke. The diesel version was slightly less powerful, but produced decidedly better economy, consuming one-third less fuel than the gasoline version. Further improving the equation was the fact that diesel fuel was a cheaper commodity already at the pump. The number series, when first introduced in 1954, sported the all-red Farmall paint scheme that had been established in the mid-thirties. After one year in the showrooms, the new Farmalls received a decorative touch of white—added as an emphasis to the radiator shell and as a backdrop to the Farmall script attached to each side of the hood. The wheels retained their combination of silver metallic rims and red spokes and hubs.

The modern era

Period of proliferation and corporate collapse

In the late fifties, influenced by trends in industrial design—automotive styling in particular—International's tractors received a major overhaul.

After having been streamlined in the forties and fifties, the look became square, projecting a bold ruggedness. And, as was the case with cars, the grille took on an importance beyond function.

But this advanced look was not an empty promise—the technological progress was spectacular. Words like Hydrostatic, Dyna-Life and Turbo really stood for things the farmer wanted and needed.

International had been cultivating markets beyond borders for decades, but now was growing truly global. In the late sixties, International could count a presence in 143 nations, including manufacturing facilities in Argentina, Australia, Brazil, England, France, Germany, Mexico and Sweden.

But by the early eighties, all was not well. The value of the dollar soared. The company had labor problems. And there was general downturn in both construction and agriculture.

In 1984, the situation became grave, and International had to divest its agricultural equipment assets. In the spring of 1985, an agreement was reached with Case, which had been able to ride the storm thanks to its Tenneco backing.

Today, while diminished in a corporate sense, the spirit of International Harvester lives on, intertwined with that of Case—a respected colleague and competitor from the pioneer days.

The products of this amalgamation will surely carry the proud tradition to future generations.

The number system introduced in the mid-fifties went crazy by the time International's tractor production reached the sixties. It was still possible to follow the logic for a while, with the one-plow 140, the two-plow 240, the three-plow 340—all new for 1958. From then on it took an expert to keep up: 404, 504, 424, 444, 544, 706, 806, 826, 656, 856, 1206. The array of numbers was dizzying and the production years overlapping. One milestone stands out in the sixties, the popular 560, an example of which is shown on the chapter opening pages, complete with a satisfied Minnesota farmer at the reins. As an example of the largest Internationals, the previous pages feature the 4786. This huge four-wheel-drive tractor follows the style introduced by International in 1966.

This first model, the 4100, was replaced by the 4166 in 1969. The modern era of tractor manufacture saw unparalleled diversification, with product lines growing in all directions, catering to big-time farmers as well as those of the garden variety—the tractors became both smaller and larger at the same time. Pictured above, the smallest of the late fifties, a Cub Cadet, contrasted with the wheels of an early giant. The utility line was distinguished by its own yellow and white paint scheme. Captured to the left—photographed on a Minnesota farm—is the International look of the eighties, characterized by strong lines and massive proportions. The 1979 tractor is an 886—a popular member of the 86 series.

On the previous pages, a tractor high on the list of milestone Internationals—the revolutionary 6788 four-wheeler with its articulated body. For the staffing of its engineering facility, which is housed in the former International complex in Hinsdale, Illinois, the new Case International organization drew on talent from both camps. The first tractor to emerge from this formidable brain trust was the 1988 Magnum series, a new line of tractors that combines the best from both worlds. The impressive heritage is certainly evident as one ponders the specifications of the newcomer, representing the new company's daring thrust into the future: new engine, new transmission, new cab, new hydraulics—all new! MFD— Mechanical Front Drive—provides more traction on demand. Digital readouts give not only data pertaining to the operation of the machine, but to area worked and area per hour, ground speed, wheel slippage and more. The series consists of four models, all six-cylinder, turbocharged diesels: the 130 hp 7110, the 150 hp 7120, the 170 hp 7130 and the 195 hp 7140, the latter sporting an intercooler. Here, the top-of-the-line Magnum shows off its attractive physiognomy accented by wraparound halogen headlights, capable of flooding the field both forward and to the sides. The Magnum is certainly a worthy successor to a long line of successes.

94

In addition to the owners of the tractors featured in this book, the author wishes to thank the following enthusiasts for their special contributions: William Anderson, Ponderosa Ranch, Incline Village, Nevada; William Cue, Antique Gas & Steam Engine Museum, Vista, California; Paul Freiling; Fred Heidrick; Norman Martin; Charles Morgantini; Manuel Neves; Kjell and Lars-Eric Sandquist, Veteran Traktor Klubben, Norrtalje, Sweden; and Kim Viker, Viker Tractor, Santa Maria, California.